LAMBERT'S
BIRDS
of Shore and Estuary

LAMBERT'S
BIRDS
of Shore and Estuary

Paintings by TERENCE LAMBERT

Text by ALAN MITCHELL

BOOK CLUB ASSOCIATES
LONDON

Acknowledgments

I would like to thank Dr John Wilson and the Natural History Department of Leicester Museum for their valuable help during the painting of this book. Without them, it could not have been done.

Terence Lambert, 1979

This edition published 1979 by
Book Club Associates
by arrangement with Wm. Collins Sons & Co. Ltd.

Contents

Introduction 7

Gulls, Terns, Skuas 14

Herring Gull 18
Blackheaded Gull 21
Great Black-backed Gull 22
Lesser Black-backed Gull 25
Common Gull 26
Kittiwake 28
Little Tern 31
Common Tern 32
Sandwich Tern 34
Great Skua 37
Arctic Skua 38

Cliff-breeding birds 40

Fulmar 42
Manx Shearwater 44
Storm Petrel 47
Gannet 49
Cormorant 50
Shag 53
Razorbill 55
Guillemot 56
Black Guillemot 58
Puffin 60
Peregrine 62
Rock Dove 65
Rock Pipit 67
Chough 69

Ducks and Geese   70

Common Scoter   73
Eider   75
Pintail   76
Mallard   79
Shelduck   80
Brent Goose   82
Barnacle Goose   84
White-fronted Goose   86

Birds of Estuaries   88

Grey Heron   91
Oystercatcher   92
Ringed Plover   94
Kentish Plover   97
Grey Plover   98
Turnstone   100
Little Stint   103
Dunlin   105
Knot   106
Ruff and Reeve   109
Sanderling   110
Redshank   112
Greenshank   115
Black-tailed and Bar-tailed Godwits   117
Curlew   119
Whimbrel   120
Avocet   123
Common Snipe   124
Reed Bunting   126

Index   128

Introduction

Land and water differ so fundamentally that their meeting is going to have some peculiarities for wildlife wherever and in whatever form it occurs. Where the water is the sea, the complications are increased by the daily changes in the level of the water as well as the nearly monthly increase and decrease in these tide levels. Diversity is the spice of wildlife and this zone where land and sea meet and mingle can provide a pattern of varied habitats which attract a greater variety of birds than is found in any other kind of landscape. A good estuary is the home of a remarkable diversity of species and where land and sea meet abruptly, at the face of a large cliff, a different but equally varied group of birds is resident; so that a great array of birds is associated with the shore—a word which, although often used to imply only a sandy beach, is taken here to mean any part of the meeting of land and sea.

In nature, two different but adjacent habitats seldom meet with a sharp boundary, but usually merge into one another over a distance. High woodland for example merges into open glade or grassland through a zone of shrubs and scrub of decreasing height. This zone is called the 'ecotone' between the habitats. The ecotone between woods and lake is alder carr and willow; the ecotone between grass and fresh water is marsh. As each habitat approaches the other, some of its plants persist over a distance but in a modified form of growth whilst other plants, adapted only to the middle zone, also appear, making the diversity of an ecotone very great in both plant and animal life. Hence broad ecotones such as marshes and extensive scrub are favourite areas for naturalists, and are exceedingly important in the world of conservation. They are also often under threat and always liable to be destroyed as 'wasteland', ideal for tipping rubbish, sewage or soil and for the passage of a bypass.

A study of a Common Gull in winter plumage. Drawn 1978.
A victim of pollution, it had taken in poison from a dump.

9

The ecotone between sea and land is the shore and varies greatly with the character and slope of the land. The breadth may be more than 1km on low, flat land, yet nil, theoretically, where a sheer cliff rises from deep water. Such cliffs are not common. Most, like Beachy Head, rise from a beach or apron of fallen rock at low tide. Those sheer into deep water are rare but occur at The Lizard, Land's End and Howth Head, Dublin. Tides at headlands are not large so that the entire ecotone may be reduced to 3m of vertical, wrack-covered rockface.

Where there is an inter-tidal zone at the foot of the cliff it may be ignored by the birds that breed on the cliff but used for feeding by Turnstones and for resting by Oystercatchers and Curlews which nest elsewhere. The Auks, Gannets, Fulmars and Choughs that nest above it feed at sea or on the cliff-tops. In this case, the ecotone between land and water is the whole of the cliff-face, which is, after all, the result of the meeting of land and sea.

The ecotone of greatest extent occurs in estuaries. Because the fall of the land is slight, the distance between high water and low water can be of great width and is increased by the enhanced tidal rise in some estuaries, notably that of the Severn where a 13m difference is found, which ranks high in the tidal rises of the world. Further, an estuary is a unique double ecotone as it is a zone of blending of land and water and of fresh and salt waters. This zone is complicated by the tides, and the changes in salinity these bring, so that the zone itself, from fresh inland water through brackish to seawater, moves up and down twice a day and further up and down at the times of spring tides than at neaps. Plants and animals, largely shellfish, crustacea and worms, therefore display subtle patterns of distribution depending on their tolerance to daily or monthly doses of brackish, salt or fresh water.

In many harbours and estuaries a mud-bank builds up with, at first, highly salt-tolerant plants, adapted to daily flooding. If mud is still being brought to the area, the plants entrap a little as each tide recedes and so the bank rises. Gradually it stands clear of more and more tides and attracts plants which grow best when flooded only a few times in a month. At low water the erosion of the mud by draining tidewater is checked by the plants and the drains or 'gutters' are localised but cut deep in intricate patterns. The bank becomes more or less stabilised as a table-land a little below the high water of spring tides or extra-high spring tides and is then almost a meadow of brackish-tolerant plants flooded only once or twice a month or only a few times each six months. These are saltings and the gutters at varying stages of the tide give food and shelter to a host of birds varying in size from Herons to Stints. During most high waters the table-tops provide an ideal resting place for thousands of waders, geese and ducks, adjacent to the mud in which they find their food and with wide views for safety. Where saltings adjoin fields, the rough ground is a nesting place for Shelduck, Redshank, Lapwing and Skylark. Saltings are centres of bird activity at all times and vital to the continued use of our coasts by vast numbers of waders and other birds. They are not desolate wastes ideal for nuclear power stations or steel-works; they hum with life in greater diversity and numbers than are found on any agricultural land.

Where low tide exposes a broad expanse of sand and strong on-shore winds are prevailing or frequent, loose sand accumulates above the high water mark. On the unstable dunes at the front only one plant can grow. Marram grass, *Psamma arenaria*, has silica-hardened blades able to withstand the erosion from continually-blown sand whilst its runners proliferate deep beneath, where it is always surprisingly moist. As the top growth increases it traps more sand and the dune rises followed by the newer growth of marram until the dune is eroded as fast as it grows, by the wind blowing out steep sided hollows. Depending upon the supply of sand and strength of winds the dune may be three or fifteen or more metres tall. By then another dune may be forming in front and so the dunes form long ranges parallel to the shore. A sizable stream draining through them will be able to keep its channel clear but some areas behind the dunes will have their drainage impeded by the ridges. Then dune 'slacks' will develop which can be long permanently damp valleys or areas of standing water. Their drainage must be by seepage under the dunes and during the highest tides the seepage can be reversed with salt water coming in, so that the slack is variably brackish.

Blown sand contains quantities of fragments of shells

pounded by the sea and these make the soil amongst and behind dunes lime-rich instead of lime-deficient and acid as are other sandy soils. These areas grow a splendid array of plants; twayblades, adder's tongue, orchids, grass of Parnassus, vetches, trefoils and violas and a great many more. The variety arises because the soils range from wet to dry, rich to poor and fresh to slightly salty, over small areas.

A well-developed slack area can be the breeding-site of Snipe, Redshank, Teal, Reed-bunting, Skylark, Linnet and a colony of Terns, whilst large areas of dune may have colonies of Herring and Lesser Black-backed Gulls. In the winter these areas are often hunted by Short-eared Owls, Merlins and Peregrine Falcons. Too many are too close to holiday centres for their own well-being. By August, when holidaymakers are most numerous the birds will have finished breeding but the plants are destroyed by too much treading, and the Spring Bank Holiday can be disastrous for the birds as well.

The outer dunes attract few birds, except during winter storms when Rock Pipits, Meadow Pipits, Snow Buntings and sometimes Shore Larks, which normally forage along the tideline, come into the dunes for shelter and to find seeds blown from the beach into hollows amongst the dunes.

The ordinary open sandy beach attracting holiday-makers is not now much used by birds in summer. When they were undisturbed, Ringed Plovers and perhaps Oystercatchers nested above the tide-line sometimes with Little Terns, but now the summer beach sees only gulls until dusk when, if the tide is suitable, some Curlew, Dunlin, Oystercatchers and Redshank may come in to feed. Out of season, however, these beaches are regular feeding places for these birds and for migrating waders such as Godwits and Sanderling, and passing parties of Terns.

Gulls, like Starlings, turn all man's activities to their advantage and swarm around harbours, piers and promenades where they may find pickings, but in the summer there are unlikely to be any more interesting birds amongst them. Only where there is a prominent headland is the holiday-maker in August in a good position to see more oceanic birds. From places like Portland Bill, Start Point, the Great Orme, Howth Head and Burghead cliffs, in August there may be sightings of passing Gannets, Fulmars, Manx Shearwaters (towards dusk) and Auks. However, beaches near rocky shores may have Cormorant, Shag and perhaps Kittiwake and Fulmar passing from time to time. Spring, autumn and even mid-winter are the times to see Petrels, Auks and Sea-duck in numbers and variety.

Gulls, Terns and Skuas

Gulls and terns are in the same family and mostly have a close general similarity, but the gulls, except perhaps the best of them, the Kittiwake, have a coarseness quite alien to the supremely elegant terns. The Kittiwake is, very properly, separated from the raffish element into a genus of its own, *Rissa*, whereas the typical gulls are all in *Larus*. All the gulls have increased inordinately in numbers during this century for a number of reasons, including a great decrease in the taking of eggs from the large colonies and increasing opportunities for scavenging at harbours, sewage outfalls (luckily now decreasing again) and rubbish dumps. They take advantage of the sanctuaries established to try to help terns to survive and since the gulls prey on tern eggs and young, one of the prime functions in the management of a tern sanctuary is to keep down the number of gulls as well as rats and dogs. Gulls nest in colonies, usually large and very noisy, on cliffs, marshes, dunes or moors. Juvenile birds are brown-speckled clumsy-looking birds and the larger the species the darker and the longer the juvenile period. The last sign of immaturity in each species is the brown band at the tip of the tail and the Great Black-backed Gull is five years old before it loses that.

The *Larus* gulls are inshore birds and all of them may follow slow ships for whatever may be thrown overboard or churned up in the wake. Only the Herring Gull is a regular follower of larger and faster ships such as modern ferries, utilising the upcurrents of air to hang with motionless wings yet progress with the ship for long periods. That the Herring Gull leaves the ship when it heads out further is only partly because it is an inshore bird. It probably could not follow a ship in this easy way if the speed exceeded about twenty knots, since a gull is not aerodynamically efficient to the degree necessary. To ride a moving 'standing wave' like that rising each side of the stern of a ship, a bird is making forward progress by a shallow dive, as it would in still air, but, by descending at exactly the rate at which the air is rising, it maintains its station. To do this requires 'penetration'—the ability to gain speed in a shallow dive and so to 'penetrate' far into still air starting from a given height. Penetration requires a wing of high efficiency, having a low 'drag' from friction with passing air but giving good lift. A long, narrow wing has this efficiency and is most fully developed in the albatrosses. The Herring Gull's wing has not this extreme efficiency and gives only moderate penetration. At slow speeds it is more than enough and the bird rides the wave behind the ship without needing the full length of wing. In fact it cannot do so with it and must furl part of the wing and ride with the inner wing raised. As the speed of the ship increases, the gull flattens and spreads its wings to their fullest extent. If the ship goes yet faster it will pass the point at which the gull can maintain its place. In order to keep up, it would have to be diving at a steeper angle and losing height faster than the air is rising, so the gull must either fall away or work by flapping its

wings to keep up. A gull riding the ship's air-wave is, of course, hoping to see something worth dropping on and eating. If it does so it must fly hard for a spell to return to the place of rest for another continuous glide. When the ship's speed calls for work to keep up and much harder work to catch up again as well, it is no longer worth the effort.

The terns are as gregarious and at least as noisy as gulls, but they are inherently graceful in every action and are dainty birds. All except the Black Terns have similar pure white and pale silvery-blue plumage with a black cap and have similar eating and nesting habits. All are summer migrants, wintering well south of the Equator and arriving from the end of March to mid May. They depart through September and early October in large mixed gatherings moving slowly south along the coast where they are harried by Skuas. A number of Common and Arctic Terns, indistinguishable in autumn, pass south via inland waters and occasionally one of these or a Little Tern wanders down the coast as late as December. The flight of a tern would be easily recognisable even if the ribbon-like wings were insufficiently distinct. In purposeful flight or chasing, the wings move through a wide arc in a flicking downstroke but apparently lazy upstroke combining to give high speed but relatively slow wing action. In normal wandering and fishing flight the flapping is shallow and mostly above the body. It is also quite rapid but progress is not and the bird careens and rolls or swings like a pendulum.

Herring Gull
Larus argentatus

This is the archetypal 'seagull' of postcards, promenades and sound-effect records. The adult in good plumage with scarlet spotted bill is very smart and, despite its blatantly avaricious eye, it is hard not to want to give food to a bird so tame as to walk up to one's feet by the harbour. The immature birds, all brown speckles, seem bigger than the adults but are the same size. The calls of Herring Gulls are many and varied. A walker on a cliff-top above nests hears most a hurried, anxious, 'wowowow' and a sharp 'wowk!' from birds sailing by, while a chorus of 'kyow-kyow-kyow' arises from below. The 'trumpet-call' is given usually from a perch and involves stretching the head forwards on an arched neck for the opening, long-drawn, 'kaaiiee-ow-', then the head thrown back for the long mocking laugh—'yockyockyockyock'. Sometimes however this is heard from birds flying high, often inland, and the contortions, although less extreme with the head kept nearly level, look odd. Now that there are inland reservoirs on which to roost, the Herring Gull will forage on farmland and follow a plough and is common around rubbish dumps. In the evening birds fly back to their roost in long flocks. Those of the middle Thames Valley have followed the same routes back to the Staines reservoirs for eighty years.

Herring Gulls squabbling over food. They have rapacious appetites, swallowing even the largest offal whole

19

Blackheaded Gull

Larus ridibundus

This gull, more than any other, belies the general term 'seagull' and is found everywhere inland throughout the year. Far from the coast it is the main plough-following bird, long having replaced the Rook. Perhaps it is less affected than the Rook by the noise and fumes of the tractors while the Rook preferred the horses. Whilst there are a few large breeding-sites on salting islands at the coast and behind dunes, there are far more high in inland mountains, on bogs at up to 700m above sea-level. About a hundred years ago the Blackheaded Gull was nearly extinct as a breeding bird but rapid and continued increase since 1900 has made that now seem beyond belief. The largest colony, at Needs Oar by the Solent, increased from ten to twenty thousand pairs between 1967 and 1972. The Blackheaded Gull has been somewhat perversely named in English and in Latin. It never has a black head. The breeding plumage, rather briefly worn, is a dark brown head and most of the year it is white. Then *ridibundus* means 'laughing' and it is hard indeed to hear any expression of amusement in the querulous, ill-tempered sounding calls of this gull, whereas the Herring Gull laughs mockingly and loud. The usual calls of the Blackheaded Gull are a harsh 'skwarr' or 'skeear' and 'kwurp'. This gull joins the ducks in city parks and can learn to feed from the hand and from office window-sills. It rests a good deal in winter on playing fields. In flight, the adult can always be distinguished from other gulls by the white leading edge to the narrow wing.

Blackheaded Gulls in summer plumage. The dark brown mask will be lost in late summer, the bird maintaining a dark spot just behind the eye

Great Black-backed Gull

Larus marinus

When in the air with other gulls this ponderous gull can be distinguished by its size and slow wing action. Adult plumage is not acquired until the birds are five years old, so that a good proportion of them are various shades of brown, like other immature gulls, and their large size is frequently the key to identification. In adult plumage this bird differs from the Lesser Black-backed in having pale pink legs and truly black back and wings. It breeds mainly on rocky coasts from the Isle of Wight west-about round to Aberdeen; there are only four sites on the east coast south of Aberdeen. As with other gulls, there has been a great increase in numbers during this century. Despite this, almost all the old inland breeding sites have been deserted in that time. This gull is now frequent in small numbers in winter far inland where it joins Herring Gulls in feeding and in the daily flights to roost on large open waters. During high water a hundred or so may settle on the higher parts of saltings with other gulls. These rapacious birds feed extensively on young Shearwaters and Puffins where they nest on the same islands, and they also take many rabbits and even cats and moles as well as eggs and young of other gulls, cormorants and ducks. Their calls are as coarse and heavy as the birds themselves and yet there is something stirring and essential to the spring day on the saltings about the deep, slow 'owk-owk-owk' that rolls over the mud and across the gutters for half a mile and hardly seems connected with those large hunched birds in the distance.

This heavily-built gull is an aggressive predator on Shearwater and Puffin colonies, turning its victims inside out

Lesser Black-backed Gull

Larus fuscus

This is the only common gull with a certain distinction; it lacks the brash, aggressive look, although its habits are in reality no better than those of the other gulls. An adult in spring has its pure white parts set off against a dark grey back and rich chrome yellow legs and can be said to be handsome, an adjective which is not readily brought to mind by gulls. This gull is the other end of a species-ring which starts with the Herring Gull and has developed a progressively darker back as it goes eastwards around the world, arriving back here as the Lesser Black-backed and ending in the Scandinavian form, which has a truly black back and is seen here mainly in winter. It lacks the contrast between the dark grey back and the black wing-tips. The Lesser Black-backed Gull breeds all down the western coasts and in a few places along the east and south coast and generally separates itself from the Herring Gull by choosing to nest on the bracken slopes and island-tops rather than the cliff-face. There are, however, many mixed colonies and many inland breeding sites especially in the north. Fifty years ago this gull was a summer migrant. By smaller inland waters it is still seen mostly passing north in February and March, sailing down slowly from a height to spend a few hours resting, or passing over in twos and threes, but now large numbers also spend the winter here, often in fields around large rubbish dumps.

Like other gulls, the Lesser Black-backed is an opportunist feeder, as happy on inland rubbish tips as on the shore

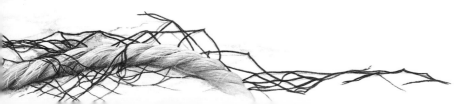

Common Gull

Larus canus

The Common Gull is common only in Scotland, where it
breeds almost throughout the country, and in northwestern
Ireland. Elsewhere there are a few colonies in the Pennines, on
Anglesey and in East Anglia and one large one, started in
1919, at Dungeness. In Scotland the nests are in small groups
by lochs, rivers and pools, and across grouse-moors, as well as
by the sea. In England and Wales it is locally common in
winter, in this plumage with the brown-streaked head. In
towns and cities it is the great football-field gull and a group
will be sitting between goal-posts every day although,
presumably, they must find somewhere else to sit on Saturday
afternoons. On the ground, this gull has a darker blue-grey
back than others and the wing-tips folded beyond the tail have
a white band vertically across them. On the open wing this
white is a prominent band in the black, formed by a large oval
'mirror' on each feather. Its dull green legs and unspotted
greenish bill also distinguish the Common Gull. Although
rather silent when sitting about, every so often one may stretch
its wings and utter a long, piercing 'kyeeeiiya' and, although
no cat has ever been heard to make a similar sound, this is
thought to be the note from which this gull has acquired the
crossword-puzzle name 'mew'. This gull is probably the one
most often seen dropping cockles or periwinkles from a height
to break their shells upon a concrete promenade. The
Common Gull seldom follows inshore ships, unlike the
Herring Gull, which habitually does so.

*A Common Gull showing the brown streaks typical of winter plumage. Preening is
particularly important in winter to preserve the insulating properties of the plumage*

Kittiwake

Rissa tridactyla

This nice bird seems altogether too refined to be a gull and it is in fact separable from the coarse *Larus* group by its lack of a hind toe. The origin of the name 'kittiwake' is apparent anywhere within earshot of a nest, from the clamorous 'kittiway-ek, kittiway-ek' calls. Away from the nesting cliffs, kittiwakes are mostly seen passing along the coast in spring and autumn, further off-shore than other gulls. At a reasonable distance they are identifiable by the uniformly black wing-tips even if the distinctive black legs cannot be seen, and by the dark blue-grey back. At great distances, and as the only gull in sight from a ship far out in the Atlantic, they are known by the flight. Flapping their bent wings slowly, they sweep in long, lazy arcs, wheeling high above the waves, then sweeping down low and up again. Immature birds have the distinctive 'tarrock' plumage, white with a black band across the back of the neck and another diagonally across each wing, as well as the usual gull's band on the end of the tail. There has been an enormous increase in Kittiwake numbers this century and now about half a million pairs breed, extending from high cliffs, previously their only home, to low cliffs and, in a few places, to buildings by tidal rivers, even those some way from the sea. At Dunbar, in Scotland, there is a colony thriving on a low ruined tower by the harbour where there are often crowds of people around the base.

Adult and juvenile Kittiwakes at the nest. These constructions of debris, algae and excrement cling precariously to the smallest cliff ledge

A Little Tern returns to the incubating female with a large sand-eel

30

Little Tern
Sterna albifrons

This tiny, graceful, very active and noisy tern has no need of its
white forehead and yellow bill to be distinct from other terns.
Were its wings not slender ribbons it would seem like a white
butterfly dancing along above the shore, careening from side
to side then hovering with wings high and flickering rapidly. It
can be heard coming from a long way off, making a high,
sharp 'kit, kit' and 'jirrik-jirrik' and long stuttering notes.
Soon after mid-April small numbers are seen along beaches on
the south and east coasts and many stay there to breed. This is
unfortunate as the beaches, spits and islands in that part of
England, from the Humber to Dorset, where two-thirds of the
British birds wish to nest, are those most used by holiday-
makers, who are a destructive influence. Hence numbers have
declined since 1930 and, in these parts, depend for their
existence increasingly on active protection. As in other terns,
the main food is sand-eels which are dived for in shallowly
covered mud or sand and can be seen held across the bill as the
bird flies to its young.

Common Tern

Sterna hirundo

This is indeed the common tern of England, Wales and Ireland, but in Britain as a whole it is outnumbered about two to one by the very similar Arctic Tern which has a large breeding population, mainly in Scotland. The Common Tern breeds all round our coasts except for a long stretch from Anglesey to Portland Bill in which the Isles of Scilly are the only station, and the coast of Yorkshire is also given a miss. It is the only tern with regular and substantial inland nesting in England and central Ireland. In England it breeds from the Midlands south-eastwards on islands in sand and gravel workings, some of which have been preserved as sanctuaries when they have been worked out. In Scotland the inland nests are on shingle banks in rivers, and on low rocky islands in lochs, where the birds will perch on the low oak trees. In autumn this is the most frequent of the terns visiting reservoirs and quite small lakes. At this time it has a white forehead and perches much on posts where, like other terns, it sits very low and holds itself level. Parties are noisy, using the contact call— a sharp 'kit, kit, kit'— and much skirling 'keer-keer-keer', also 'skeeeah', which last distinguishes it by ear from the Sandwich Tern with its grating 'keerrik'. Normal flight is peculiarly buoyant and erratic with rapid flicks of the slender angular wings, but these birds are much given to chasing, when progress is fast and direct. When fishing they fly slowly and level some ten metres above the water and dive rapidly, often after hanging for a few seconds tilted up with the tail down.

Common Terns are capable of hovering even in a strong wind, holding their heads down, scanning the water below

Sandwich Tern
Sterna sandvicensis

The biggest of the terns, except for the very rare Caspian Tern, the Sandwich Tern is also the first to arrive here in spring. At many places along the coast the first birds will be seen passing, often close inshore, as early as the third week in March, returning from a winter on the coasts of South Africa. The small parties moving along the coast have periods of silence, but frequent outbreaks of the skirling cries general to terns, like 'kreeah-kreeah-kreeah' and 'kitkitkit', will include the one call, easily known, which distinguishes this tern from all others. This is loud, harsh and grating but oddly with a well-oiled quality, 'Keerrik!'. It is occasionally heard inland from the night sky. Nesting is on shingle and sand bars and low salting islands and, as with other terns, storms and extra high tides cause disastrous losses of eggs and young, as can disturbance by man, fox or dog during the peak of activity amongst the crowded nests. Well-protected sanctuaries, sometimes with control of numbers of gulls, have brought about a modest increase in breeding pairs since 1920. By midsummer the adults have begun their moult, acquiring a white forehead, and by autumn the black head has become speckled black or grey on white. The crest at the nape has disappeared by autumn. Even in spring this was not very noticeable in flight but on a perched bird it can often be raised by the wind even when not deliberately used in display. In any plumage the Sandwich Tern is less ribbon-winged and more gull-like than the other terns and is identifiable by its heavy bill, which is black with a pale yellow tip, and by shorter less slender streamers on the tail, as well as the 'keerrik' call. It also chases about rather less than other terns and dives more heavily.

In late summer, before setting out on autumn migration, the white above the bill of this Sandwich Tern will extend above the crown

Great Skua
Stercorarius skua

This is the only seabird which breeds in both the north
Atlantic and the Antarctic regions. Except for wanderers
which may meet around the Equator, the populations are
separate although indistinguishable in the field. The small
northern population breeds only on Iceland, the Faeroe
Islands and in the far north of Scotland. More than half of the
Scottish birds breed on Foula, a remote Shetland island, and
Shetlanders have always known it by the Viking name 'Bonxie'
which is a good name with which to distinguish all the North
Atlantic birds from the Antarctic ones. Since 1890 the colonies
on Foula and on Unst have been protected. This has allowed
the number of nests to increase from scarcely one hundred to
well over 2000 and for small colonies to spread throughout the
Orkneys and to the mainland. Formerly the eggs were taken
for food and then for collections. Around the coast elsewhere
small numbers are seen passing, mostly in autumn along the
east coast. Seen at a distance a bird may be dismissed as yet
another of the dark immature large gulls unless the rather
broader wings, short tail and short bill are noticed, then, if the
wings are spread, the large white patch on the outer wing
which is the best mark of identity. However, if the bird goes in
pursuit of a gannet, gull or tern its flight pattern becomes
almost like that of a falcon with purposeful and powerful
strokes of angled wings and rapid turns and twists. Great
Skuas have been seen upsetting gannets in flight by seizing the
tip of the wing or tail in its bill. When a tern or gull being
chased is scared into dropping a fish the skua often catches the
food before it hits the water. Skuas also often eat adult puffins
which they catch outside their burrows or in flight.

Herring Gull chicks left unattended are easy prey for the Great Skua

Arctic Skua

Stercorarius parasiticus

This bird has two different forms, the light and the dark. The light is a handsome, cream-faced, white-bellied bird which predominates in the northern Arctic colonies but to the south, even in Shetland, the most northerly British station, it is outnumbered about six to one by dark forms. The typical dark form is even darker than the Great Skua and deserves the name 'skua', meaning dark (as found in 'ob-scure'), but somewhat paler-faced intermediate forms are frequent. Small numbers breed on Jura, some on the Outer Hebrides and in Sutherland and there has been a small steady increase in numbers. Even so the entire British population is little above a thousand pairs, making this the rarest breeding seabird here. In September and October birds from the Arctic join the Shetland and Orkney birds migrating south along the east coast and this is when Arctic Skuas are seen most, accompanying and preying upon the thousands of terns and Kittiwakes passing along the coast. In places where the terns linger and circle, as in the Firth of Forth below the bridges, the skuas often rest on the water in the intervals between feeding, three or four together, sitting high in the water and looking like dark immature gulls until they rise and start into pursuit. Intruders on the nesting site of this bird, whether animal or human are attacked from behind and may be struck by the feet or the tips of the wings. Dogs have been seen to be scratched with the claws.

A light-phase Arctic Skua, superbly adapted for high-speed pursuit of other birds which it robs of their prey

Cliff-breeding birds

The singularities of a sea-cliff bring together a mixture of birds that breed there to utilise the different features. Facing erosion from the sea, such a cliff is more fractured, with caves and with more crevices than an inland cliff. They are needed by the Chough, Black Guillemot and Rock Dove in particular and are an added attraction to many other birds. A sea-cliff, especially one rising from deep water, is, in general, less accessible to predators and disturbing invaders, human and canine, than any other kind of site. This provides essential protection for the very vulnerable colonies like those of Guillemot and Razorbill and is useful to the Peregrine Falcon, Fulmar and Shag. Equally, the fallen rocks and boulders at the cliff foot provide a secure resting place for the Rock Pipit. Best of all is a sea-cliff rising sheer within gliding range of deep water which is the only possible nesting site for birds of which the young or the adults cannot alight on land, walk about freely on it or take off from it. All the Auks, Petrels and Shearwaters are in this group with, to a lesser extent, the Fulmar, Shag and Cormorant.

The loose screes, slopes with light soils and little plateaux amongst the cliffs have three features of value or even of necessity to some birds. They allow the making of burrows which are fairly inaccessible and from the mouths of which direct descent to the sea is possible. Here, therefore, live the Puffins, Petrels and Shearwaters. The fractured cliff-face will, if the rock of which it is made has its beds reasonably level in alignment, provide the ledges on which the Guillemots, Razorbills, Kittiwakes and Fulmars crowd whilst many are also used by the Herring Gull which can perfectly well nest in many other places. This crowding of some of the possible prey of the Peregrine Falcon and Great Skua makes the cliffs even more attractive to those birds.

The remaining site-type associated with cliffs is the cliff-top table-land which is not cliff at all but depends for its features

and use by birds on being surrounded by cliff. Small rocky
islands are where it is found at its best. It combines relative
inaccessibility with closeness to deep water and adjacence to
colonies of other birds. The birds nesting on cliff-tops either
make nests in the open, notably the Gannet, Great and Arctic
Skuas, Herring and Lesser Black-backed Gull, or make or use
burrows as do the Storm and Leach's Petrels and Manx
Shearwater, and Puffin.

41

Fulmar

Fulmarus glacialis

This petrel is of particular interest for its effortless flight and for its huge increase in numbers and spread in breeding in this century. When flying amongst gulls, the Fulmar is conspicuous in holding its wings quite straight and level from root to tip, without the angle at the joint so prominent in the gulls. On rigid wings it glides for long periods, passing rapidly along a cliff face, using the updraught from the wind to achieve lift. Only occasionally does it need to flap its wings and then does so with a few quick, markedly shallow strokes.

A passing Fulmar has a dove-like appearance from its rounded head and soft plumage and the typical petrel bill, seemingly made of bits and pieces glued roughly together, is visible. This, with the small black patch in front of the eye, and the pale-ended wings often with a light brown middle distinguishes it from any gull.

Until 1878 Fulmars bred only on the remote islands of St Kilda. In that year they spread to the Shetlands and Sutherland had its first in 1903. Now there are some 300,000 nests and every rocky cliff-face has at least a few. This expansion is achieved despite a clutch rigidly fixed at a single egg, never replaced after loss, and birds having to reach seven years old before breeding. However, the mean expectation of life is at least sixteen years and some may live to be more than forty.

Fulmars are subject to subtle colour variations, from the light grey phase shown here, to a more 'blue' phase

Manx Shearwater
Puffinus puffinus

The naming of this bird has become a little tangled. It has not bred on the Isle of Man for about 180 years and it is, as its Latin names show, the true Puffin. This name, however, has been transferred to that colourful auk, although it does not have as extended a 'puffin' stage as that of the Shearwater. A young Shearwater hatches after seven weeks and is then fed for another seven until it is twice the weight of the adult. It is then a 'puffin', is deserted by its parents and lives only on its fat for another week. The parents have fed it on pilchards and sprats caught hundreds of miles away; a few from Skokholm off South Wales feeding off North Spain. Manx Shearwaters have been found to have strong homing abilities even when taken across the Atlantic Ocean and one returned 3000 miles from Boston to Wales in $12\frac{1}{2}$ days.

The Shearwaters as a group derive their name from their manner of flight. They skim along just above the flanks of a wave, keeled over so that one wing-tip almost cuts the water, then swing over with the other wing down. The Manx Shearwater, being black above and clear white beneath, flashes black and white at each turn. It is seen flying off-shore or in packs resting on the water by day and comes to land only at night as it is a favourite prey of the Great Black-backed Gull. It nests in deep warrens of burrows on suitable cliff-tops on islands off the west and north coasts of Britain and Ireland.

The long, narrow wings of the Manx Shearwater enable the birds to travel vast distances with the minimum of effort

Storm Petrel

Hydrobates pelagicus

'Mother Carey's Chicken' is a tiny bird to meet far out in the ocean—about the size of the House Martin which its black upper side and white rump call to mind. The white patch is however a well curved arc and the black tail is visibly round-ended. In good plumage a line of pearly white dots forms a wing-bar. You may occasionally see one fluttering along in the wake of a ship in the eastern North Atlantic or in the Mediterranean but you are lucky if a spring sea-watch turns up one heading for its breeding ground in May. The one time when several may be seen in estuaries, harbours and off-shore is when a strong October or November gale catches the large numbers moving south off the west coasts and blows them eastwards to the land. The worst storms coming at the critical time cause a 'wreck', for many Petrels are blown inland where such oceanic birds are lost in a foreign element. Their way of dipping the bill in flight to take surface plankton brings them nothing useful in fresh water, apart from a few insects, so that, unless they quickly regain the sea, they starve. Dead birds are found scattered across the country after a 'wreck'.

Nesting colonies ranging from a few pairs to more than ten thousand, are found from Shetland down the west coast of Scotland, Ireland and Wales to the Scilly Isles and the Channel Isles, the nests being in crevices in walls, cliffs and rocks or in scrapes and burrows.

Storm Petrels follow in the wake of ships, finding food brought to the surface by the propeller's disturbance

Gannet
Sula bassana

The Gannet belongs to the same order of birds as the Pelican but in its naming has popularly been associated with the Goose. It is, or was, called the Solan Goose, Solan with *Sula* coming from the Icelandic name for the bird, and Gannet itself is related to 'gander'. The descriptive name *'bassana'*, is from the Bass Rock, a big gannetry east of Edinburgh. This big bird has a two-metre wing-span and is one metre from bill-tip to tail. A feeding flock of a hundred or more birds is a great spectacle. The adults flashing pure white, cream and black and the immature birds nearly black, they wheel about, 30–40m above a shoal of fish and pour down into the sea. Each bird turns sharply and half folds its wings, with the tips pointing straight out behind, and dives at an angle of about 45 degrees sending up a big splash as it hits the water. Gannets can often be seen passing a fair way out from headlands, beating low over the water in small groups flying line-ahead. Their long narrow wings with prominent black tips give several lazy flaps between long glides while frequent rolls show the full upper side.

About three-quarters of the entire population of some 200,000 pairs of this North Atlantic bird breed in the British Isles, all on off-shore stacks and islets except for a small colony started in 1937 on Bempton Cliffs, Yorkshire. The total number of pairs in Britain has trebled during this century.

Flocks of wheeling Gannets are often seen in the distance in pursuit of shoals of fish. Against a dark sky, the black wing tips give the impression that the wings have been 'chopped' short

Cormorant

Phalacrocorax carbo

Few birds can be less like a crow than the Cormorant but just
because it is mainly black it was 'sea-crow' to the Romans,
'*corvus marinus*' and hence 'Cormorant'. It ranges widely
across the world from eastern Canada to Japan and New
Zealand. It has a primitive, reptilian look about it, particularly
when sitting as it often does, low in the water with curved neck
and raised bill separated from that part of its back which is
above the water, or with nothing else showing. It will then dive
either by putting its head down and sinking out of sight or by
jumping almost clear of the water. It rests much between feeds
and does so perched on a rock, post or, in places, a tree, with
its wings held out. It seems that the wings need to be dried in
this way as they lack adequate water-proofing, which, for a
bird which must feed under water, makes the bird seem as
ridiculous as it often looks. A line of twenty birds in this
position on adjacent posts on a jetty is an odd sight.
Cormorants often feed inland on large rivers and reservoirs
and there are a few nesting colonies on inland cliffs but not far
from the sea. Many roosts are much further inland, sometimes
on buildings or trees and the birds fly high to reach them, the
wings moving in a shallow arc and flapping rapidly for their
size.

*Only during the early spring, when Cormorants breed, are the white chin and thigh
patches so well defined as shown here*

Shag

Phalacrocorax aristotelis

This smaller edition of the Cormorant rarely seems to wear the crest from which it is named. In the winter it is not yet in breeding plumage and before full summer it is back in winter dress. Identification usually depends on the Shag's size, more rapid wing-action and lack of white on the head and thigh. Young birds also differ from Cormorant young in not having a white belly. Seen in good light at no great distance the Shag shows the green gloss and bright yellow gape which are distinctive features. At close range the adults show emerald-green eyes. Over 30,000 pairs of Shags breed on the coasts of Great Britain and Ireland, the greater part of them in Scotland while there is only one small station in Yorkshire between the Farne Islands and the Isle of Wight. In some winters many are seen along that stretch of the east coast and a few on big rivers and lakes inland, but it is really a bird of rocky coasts and cliff-edged islands. Sitting low in the water between dives, the Shag returns below the surface by sinking quietly much less often than by a leap well clear of the surface, flexing its body in a graceful arc to follow the bill and head without a splash.

A problem with an exposed cliff nest site is one of over-heating. Young Shags are shaded by the brooding parents' outstretched wings and 'panting' also aids heat loss

Razorbill

Alca torda

From early January until late May a Razorbill or two may be seen flying past any headland, low over the waves, black and white and bustling, with regular rapid wing-beats. From July until the end of the year more may similarly be seen, dispersing in the autumn, perhaps wandering gently back to their cliffs in the winter. In between they are confined to the waters around the cliffs where they breed. These must, as far as possible, be inaccessible to man, dogs, foxes and other animals, and have ledges, or slab type boulders beneath for nesting. Such sites are numerous around Ireland, Scotland and the west coast. From The Needles to the Borders on the east coast, only Bempton and Flamborough Head in Yorkshire attract Razorbills. Silent at sea, Razorbills use many calls at the nest, particularly a very low-frequency growl but also a Raven-like 'rruk', 'oort' and a 'woop-woop' like a Stock-dove. When flying Razorbills use all the surface area they have in order to gain the necessary lift — wings fully extended, small tail spread. Coming in to the cliff ledge they swing their bodies to the vertical so that wing action drives upwards not forwards, and the body and tail create drag to slow them down as they sweep up from below, an approach which cannot be used for water. When they slow down to alight they cannot compensate for failing lift by increasing area, and just plunge into the water. They swim fast beneath the water when fishing, using the wings in short quick strokes.

Razorbills, in common with many of the auks, have legs set well back and rest using their tarsus, the lower part of their leg, giving them this typical upright stance

Guillemot
Uria aalge

The Guillemot probably owes its name not to a French
'William' but to 'gull' and 'mew' implying a doubly wailing
bird. It is the most numerous nesting seabird in these islands
with well over half a million pairs. The general range is exactly
that of the Razorbill, with the same gap from The Needles to
Bempton and from there to Scotland, but the colonies tend to
be fewer and larger. Many are shared with the Razorbill.
There are two forms and one variant involved in our
population. From mid-Scotland northwards, the northern
form, nearly as black as the Razorbill, replaces the browner
southern form. In both groups a 'ringed' or 'bridled' variant
occurs with, as in the picture, a white ring round the eye and
narrowly extending back to the neck. In Cornwall only one
per cent of the birds is bridled but this increases northwards
and about a quarter of those in the Shetlands have this smart
trimming. Bridled birds are thus distinct from the similar
Razorbill but it is not a feature that shows from afar. The
southern form is distinctly brown and white rather than black
and white but with the northern form the points to note are the
tapered bill and, especially noticeable as they sit on the water,
the longer more slender neck, and in flight a much less
prominent white trailing edge to the wing than in the
Razorbill. In winter plumage both species have white from
chin almost to the nape. Auks do not come inland deliberately,
but may be driven in by storms. They cannot feed on inland
waters so must return to the sea as soon as they are able.

*From April onwards, Guillemots crowd on the breeding ledges forming colonies of
many thousands*

Black Guillemot

Uria grylle

'Black Guillemot' is something of an ornithological name for a
bird known in the far north and wherever Vikings roved by the
Old Norse name 'Tystie' which perhaps derives from the bird's
call. It is also known as 'dovekie', especially when in its winter
plumage with barred black and white upper parts, and this
name combines the dove-like appearance at that time with the
connected meaning of 'diver'. In summer it is all black except
for its big white wing patches. It is easily recognised in either
plumage and there is something inescapably appealing about
this small auk with its red feet and its little bo'sun's pipe
whistle. It breeds in small numbers all round Ireland and from
Anglesey and the Isle of Man northwards but there are none
on the east coast except in the far northern corner of Scotland.
Where they inhabit tall cliffs they remain near the bottom, in
caves and crevices and among fallen cliff segments. If you lie
face downward on the top of the 100m sandstone cliffs at
St Bees, Cumbria, you can watch them flying to and fro,
sitting on the water and diving from the surface with wings
bent into a right-angle, and in the clear water there you can see
the red legs being used underwater. The shrill 'tseep' call rises
from far below. In some parts, Black Guillemots have taken to
nesting in holes in piers and harbour walls and in rabbit holes.
They leave the nesting area in July but move off-shore rather
than southward and are little seen on the south and east coasts
of England.

*An alert Black Guillemot in summer plumage. When at rest, the bird shows a stouter
neck*

Puffin

Fratercula arctica

The English name, Puffin has been borrowed from the Shearwaters (as explained on page 44) whilst '*Fratercula*' means 'little brother' and refers to its monastic dress, although it looks more like one of today's nuns. Most people are familiar with the appearance of the adult in breeding plumage but it is not widely known that in winter the blue-grey adornments above and below the eye and much of the yellow by the mouth and the base of the bill are shed; the bill itself becomes mainly yellow and is reduced in size and the cheeks and throat become grey. Even in winter it is easy to identify as it flies past, as a small auk with a deep triangular bill and a nearly white face. In juveniles the face is the important feature since the bill is then about a third as deep as in the adult and is all dark brown. Puffins do not nest on rocky ledges or in crevices like other auks but they use burrows in the soil on slopes above and among the cliffs and in screes. Rabbit holes and Manx Shearwater burrows can be taken or new burrows made. Some large colonies have so loosened the soil by constant mining that erosion is making the slopes less and less suitable. There are a few colonies in Dorset and along the west coast but the greater part of the still large, but apparently declining, population nests on islets off the coast of Scotland. The Puffin stands more upright and walks better than other auks which adds to its quaintly human air. Under water, the Puffin swims rapidly using its wings. In flight the wings work very fast but in shallow strokes giving the typical auk's almost bee-like progress, buzzing straight and low over the water.

Puffins in summer plumage. Sand-eels are held to the upper mandible by the Puffin's tongue. In this way up to a dozen fish may be caught and held

Peregrine Falcon

Falco peregrinus

This splendid bird has the high-performance wings of the falcon. They are well developed with long slender tips of strongly muscled primary feathers and in pursuit flight are driven with a whip-lash effect giving the bird great speed. Even greater speeds are attained during the 'stoop' when it dives to the kill. This is the acme of fast flight in birds and is a power-dive with the long wings bent back close to the body and the primaries driving the bird down faster than gravity alone can achieve. At these speeds the passage of the bird causes a loud hissing. This will often attract attention to a brief event that otherwise is easy to miss. The Peregrine suffered some destruction during World War Two because it could have proved a hazard to pigeons carrying distress messages and none has since nested along the coasts of Sussex and Hampshire. Recovery afterwards was halted by the spreading use of certain pesticides and by 1963 numbers were at their lowest. But, with the partial bans on the use of these chemicals, a slow recovery continues and about 400 pairs breed, mainly in Scotland and Cumbria with some in Wales and Ireland. Around the nest the male can be noisy and often sits on a prominence and calls, 'chak-chak-chak-chok-chok-chak'.

Peregrines prey upon the huge flocks of waders overwintering on saltings. The rapid flight of the Dunlin is no match for the stoop of the falcon

Rock Dove

Columba livia

All the town, racing and domestic pigeons have been bred from the Rock Dove. In most gatherings in a city square there will be some birds which show this origin, for the 'Blues' or 'Blue Rocks' with two broad black bands across the wings and a white rump have retained the plumage. Unfortunately, however, it is not only this form but all kinds of bizarre black, brown and white forms which spread from coastal towns to join and soon replace the true Rock Doves nesting along the cliffs. Probably no colony is without this motley brigade of hangers-on and true Rock Doves now predominate only on the remoter cliffs of the west and north of Scotland and Ireland. These birds breed in caves in coastal cliffs while the colonies on inland cliffs are all feral pigeons which also nest on buildings. Rock Doves, true and adulterated, feed together on rough pasture and in ploughed fields sitting low like Stock Doves and sometimes with them, but looking much greyer and less blue. In most parts, the presence of chequered and particoloured birds identifies them. The wild birds have a long breeding season, laying two or three clutches from April to August, but the feral forms in towns lay five or more throughout the year. The low cooing song, which is the same in wild and feral birds is heard at any time of the year.

The Rock Dove, ancestor of the familiar feral Pigeon whose plumage may often be identical

Rock Pipit
Anthus spinoletta

The Rock Pipit seems a more substantial, less flittery bird than the Meadow Pipit which, in winter, will often frequent the same parts of the shore. It is 1cm longer but looks larger and its flight is dashing rather than flitting, although it does have a bounding, dipping flight when travelling any but small distances. It sweeps over a breakwater with a strong sharp single 'tseeep' to land on tideline wrack and search for kelp-flies, sand-hoppers or seeds. It breeds in tumbled boulders at the foot of cliffs or in hollows in the face of low cliffs all round the coast except in Morecambe Bay and East Anglia which lack suitable sites. In winter it spreads to saltings and beaches without cliffs, sometimes in small parties but usually only one or two at a time. It is very rarely seen inland or perching on trees: the pipit seen inland in winter which gives the same single note when disturbed and flies into a tree is the Alpine form, the Water Pipit. The Rock Pipit gives its full song in soaring and descending flight. Starting, as it rises, with accelerating 'tseep' notes it changes on the descent to longer notes, then a long hard rattle. On the ground this bird walks, like other pipits, whereas other small birds hop.

Rock Pipit with a bill full of kelp and Muscid fly, collected from the tideline seaweed

Chough

Pyrrhocorax pyrrhocorax

A crow which is so aberrant as to have a scarlet curved bill almost deserves to be classified, as the Chough was by Linnaeus, as a form of Hoopoe. Its only close relative is the Alpine Chough which has a shorter yellow bill but shows eccentricity in its high-pitched little chirruping notes. The Chough was associated with Cornwall and called the Cornish Daw but it has not bred there since 1952 although a single bird remained at one cliff area throughout 1977. Before 1910 it bred on cliffs along the south coast as far east as Sussex. At present it is confined to the Isle of Man, north and west Wales, southern and western Ireland, northern Ireland and the island of Islay. The note from which the Chough has acquired its name ('chow') is 'kyeeow' starting with greater abruptness than the Jackdaw's similar note, more musical, and drawn out to an indistinct end. The Chough is a glorious flier, sweeping, diving and soaring along cliff-faces with complete mastery of the air and can do the Raven's trick of rolling over on its back. The usual places for a nest are in caves and crevices in cliffs but some ruined or disused buildings are regularly occupied and the few inland birds use old mineshafts. The feeding habits of the Chough are somewhat unexpected for, despite its dependence nearly everywhere on coastal cliffs, it is not a tideline feeder; it feeds on close-grazed turf and rough ground around the cliffs. This is where that slender curved bill comes in, for in the breeding season the birds rely on a diet of ants and their larvae and the bill is an adaptation for probing.

Sheep not only supply nest-lining but their close cropping of grass increases the number of ant colonies upon which Chough feed

Ducks and Geese

Ducks, geese and swans are all in one large family, which shows how closely they are related to one another. Swans are readily distinguished from geese, despite a bird called the Swan Goose which is obviously a goose, not because they are white (remember the Black Swan), but because their size, slender neck and the fact that the feet are tucked away under the stern. Geese and ducks are less readily separable because of the group of shelducks which share some of the features of geese. As in geese, male and female shelducks are hard to tell apart, and both groups have their legs forward under the mid-belly enabling them to walk easily and stand grazing with the body held level.

Geese in this part of the world can usefully be divided into grey and black geese. The grey geese are birds of farm-lands rather than the coast although in hard weather and often at other times a number may frequent saltings, and the White-fronted Goose is usually not far from a tidal river. It is the grey geese which flight at dawn and dusk in huge, clamorous skeins. (In the air, geese are in 'skeins', pronounced 'skeens', no connection with hanks of wool; on the ground they are in 'gaggles'.) The black geese, the Barnacle and Brent, are entirely coastland birds, rarely wandering inland. They are black and

white whereas grey geese are brown and white with, in Grey Lag and Pink-footed, a blue-grey area on the inner wing. The black, or sea-geese are governed in their daily movements by the tides and also move in skeins of thousands with yelping or barking calls. The Brent is a bird of salt marshes and the Barnacle of more local occurrence, mainly on smaller salt marshes along rocky shores.

The Shelduck is the typical estuary bird, liking mud, salting and rough grass by the sea and usually seen in hundreds together by any large estuarial system. The other ducks can be divided into dabblers and divers, more usually put as surface-feeding and diving ducks. This is a rather coarse division and diving ducks include some separable as sea-ducks—Eiders, Scoters and Long-tailed Duck. The Common Eider and Common Scoter are rather heavily built ducks at home in rough waters. The Mallard is the typical surface-feeding duck and is equally found by any inland waters and marshes as well as in estuaries but the Pintail, closely related to the Mallard is markedly a duck of saltings and is especially likely to be seen in an area which is frequented by geese—that is, the more open and extensive grasslands and saltings and nearby marshes.

Common Scoter

Melanitta nigra

This bird's name is the same word as 'scooter' and seems to have been acquired from the display behaviour often seen in small flocks when there is much 'speedboating' in short dashes, raising spray, or perhaps from the long, splashing take-off. A string of Common Scoter flying low over the sea is easily recognised by the mixture of entirely black drakes and dark brown ducks, with pale faces visible at a fair distance and all with unmarked wings. Common Scoter often fly in small tightly bunched groups of about twenty birds in a globular cluster. Where they are in hundreds, a complete raft of them may rise from the sea as one body and fly in a broad mass, few from back to front but many deep. An active group at fairly close quarters may be heard to be making a rippling 'titititi' call. In spring and autumn fair numbers are seen passing headlands on all coasts and a few, mostly females, turn up on inland waters. During the winter smaller numbers frequent some bays and estuaries. Less than two hundred pairs nest in the British Isles, scattered thinly from Caithness to County Mayo, in heather a short distance from freshwater lochans or on islands in larger lochs. They have spread slowly southwards and have recently bred on Loch Lomond. Their numbers have increased in Ireland so that two-thirds of all the nests in the British Isles are now there. At sea it feeds mainly on mussels, and on fresh water it eats snails and insect larvae but also parts of water plants.

Common Scoter rarely leave the sea but occasionally rest on isolated rocky promontories and sandbanks. Only the male has the orange bill stripe, females are brown with white cheeks and throats

Eider
Somateria mollissima

A string of rather dark, heavy looking ducks flying low over the sea, each with white patches in different places, can only be Eiders. The young drakes present a great array of patterns of black and white throughout the year and it is the immature birds which are most often seen passing in areas distant from the breeding colonies. The adult drake is a striking example of reverse colouring, black below and white above, which is very rare throughout the animal kingdom where the upper side is almost always dark and the underside is white or pale. The apple-green of the back of his head is a very rare colour on northern birds and the combination with the pale orange on the breast is not found in any other British bird. From nesting on only a few islands in Scotland in 1850, the Eider has increased and spread enormously. It now nests on nearly every suitable stretch of coast in Scotland and, since 1912, in many places in the north of Ireland. There is an increasing new colony on Walney Island, Cumbria whilst the Farne and Coquet Islands off Northumberland have long been important breeding places. Until about 1950 it was rare to see an Eider along the coasts of southern England but immature birds are now quite frequent off the east and south coasts and these probably derive from the Dutch colonies which have increased greatly since that time.

Eiders feed by diving to the bottom for molluscs.

Adult drake Eiders take up to four years to attain full breeding plumage. During the time the females are incubating, the drakes leave the breeding area forming large bachelor groups

Pintail

Anas acuta

This elegant and beautiful bird is numerous in winter only in coastal areas that attract geese also. On these saltings and estuaries there may be pairs or small groups feeding and flying with, but not really among, flocks of Wigeon, or there may be two hundred or more in their own flock. When feeding in numbers some drakes usually stand with their heads high, making the pure white on the neck and running up the side of the head very conspicuous. The female, seen on its own is separable from a female wild duck by its slender, elongated body and wings, paler colour and the pale border to the hind edge of the wing. The speculum is much less prominent and is brownish green. Since 1915 when it bred only in a few areas in Scotland the Pintail has spread as a breeding bird and many more now breed in the Fens and in Kent than in the north. The number breeding is however tiny in comparison with the flocks from Scandinavia and Russia arriving on the northeast coast during October and spreading to all the favoured sites by December. When there are high spring tides Pintail may rest on the sea or in mid-estuary. Even on fairly short flights they tend to fly high and very fast with shallow wing-beats making an audible swishing sound. The central pair of tail feathers on the drake may be 10cm longer than the others and at rest they are held at a rising angle, often blown by the wind into a curve over the back.

An adult drake Pintail, one of the most elegant of ducks

Mallard

Anas platyrhyncha

The name for the drake of the Wild Duck has been adopted for the species as a whole. 'Mallard' implies 'the very male one' and is derived from the reprehensible activities of the drake which chases other females when his mate is confined to brooding the eggs. Truly wild Wild Duck are wary and may spend the day at sea or on floodwater and lakes, coming into fields to feed only by night, but nonetheless this is the first duck to be attracted by the easy living in a town park where it becomes very confiding. This is the duck which, fully domesticated, has given rise to the farmyard ducks, Aylesbury and Rouen Runner. These forms all show their origin by the upcurled two pairs of central tail feathers in the drake. In wild birds flying these feathers can often be seen from a distance identifying the birds at once. The duck, not the drake, is responsible for the descending series of quacks which burst out loudly and often; the drake has only a conversational 'reeb, reeb' or 'quek, quek' which is heard a great deal from birds being fed on a park lake. On the inner wing both birds have a broad bar of iridescent purple or green, the colour depending on the light. This speculum is present in varying colours on other dabbling ducks and usefully identifies each in flight, especially during the extensive summer moult. In breeding plumage the drake displays a green head, shot with purple towards moult, and a purple-brown breast, separated by a white collar, with a grey back and underparts. When in 'eclipse' the drakes are very like the speckled brown ducks but are distinguished by their yellow bills.

Within hours of hatching, Mallard ducklings are foraging with the parent duck

Shelduck
Tadorna tadorna

This fine bird is a link between the ducks and the geese and is goose-like in its level stance on forward placed legs. The word 'sheld' seems to mean 'particoloured' but is related to 'shield' and is thus apt for the bright orange pattern on white when this bird is seen from the front. Shelduck are commonly seen lining the seaward edge of saltings where, from a distance, they make a bright white line, much whiter than a similar mass of gulls. Many estuaries hold four or five hundred birds and a few hold a thousand but not in late summer. At that time the birds are moulting and this is a sudden and complete moult so that flight is impossible for a few weeks. Birds in the southwest gather on sandbanks in Bridgwater Bay for the moult but the rest all go to the Heligoland Bight around the island of Sylt. Shelduck breed in burrows, haystacks, broken walls and in trees and have spread inland recently in East Anglia. When they go away to moult, many parent birds leave their young in the charge of those that remain, and large parties of chicks are shepherded to the water, often across roads where they may need co-operation from sympathetic motorists.

A female Shelduck emerges from the rabbit burrow in which she has built her nest. Drakes look the same but, in summer, usually develop a knob on the upper bill

Brent Goose

Branta bernicla

The name 'brent', implying a burnt or charred colour, aptly characterises this bird, especially the dark-breasted form which breeds in Greenland and Canada and is the one seen off the south coast of England and is predominant in eastern Britain. The pale-breasted form breeds from Spitsbergen to West Siberia and is the form wintering in Ireland and in some of west Scotland. Often seen in small groups flying along the coast low above a rough sea, the Brent Goose at first looks like a heavy duck with its rapid wing-beat and small size. When it is alongside the bright white under the stern is prominent and the white flecks on the dark neck also show well. Retreating birds show the 'black goose' pattern of black rump and tail separated by a white arc. Fifty years ago the Brent fed largely on the marine plant 'Wigeon grass' or *Zostera* and was seen only where that was plentiful. A disease destroyed much of the *Zostera* and Brent numbers declined seriously. Shooting them was made illegal and numbers rose steadily until now the big Essex and Sussex wintering grounds have more than 10,000 birds each and these are now starting to feed on meadow-grasses. At high tide the birds crowd on to uncovered salting and as the tide retreats they move into the gutters, hundreds rising at a time in noisy formless skeins for short, low flights. The chorus is largely made up of a deep single note, 'krowk'.

Dark-breasted Brent Geese feeding on the seaweed Enteromorpha *at low tide*

Barnacle Goose

Branta leucopsis

The appearance of the word 'barnacle' here and in the
scientific name of the Brent Goose reflects the ancient belief
that these arctic-breeding sea-geese, whose nests were then
unknown, grew out of barnacles. Elaborate engravings were
made showing every stage. The popularity of this myth is said
to owe much to the idea that with such an origin these birds
must really be fish and thus could be eaten on fast-days. This
goose winters in large flocks only in a few places in Scotland,
notably on the Dumfries coast of the Solway and in the Inner
Hebrides. Single birds appear at times with other geese
elsewhere, mostly in severe weather, but some of these stay
behind when the main body migrate northwards and these are
injured birds, mostly carrying shot. Otherwise this goose tends
to be in flocks of its own kind alone. It is considerably less
wary when on the ground than are other geese. The calls are
short rapid barks, so a skein flying over sounds somewhat like
a pack of hounds in cry. Breeding was first discovered in
Spitsbergen and is known only in a small part of Greenland
and on the west Siberian coast and islands.

Barnacle Geese, grazing on rough coastal grassland

White-fronted Goose

Anser albifrons

Although named for its white forehead, this goose is most readily identified in the field by the big black irregular bars on its underside. The white on the head can be seen only from close-to in flight or in good light on birds on the ground, but in a skein flying over there will always be some adults showing the barring clearly from below. This is a goose of large areas of grassland in broad valleys as much as of saltings and is the only grey goose regularly found in suitable areas along the south coast of England. The often-flooded grazing by the River Avon west of the New Forest normally holds about 3,000 birds and the Arun Valley in Sussex attracts a good number, especially during floods. These birds arrive in late November and leave in early March. Up to 10,000 or more gather then on the saltings at Slimbridge by the Severn and move north to the Ribble Estuary in Lancashire. In hard weather small parties leave the flocks and forage in less extensive but otherwise similar areas so that two or three birds may be found on grazing and floods behind sea-walls. Wexford Slob in Ireland is the winter quarters for many thousands, mainly from Greenland. The calls of this goose are distinctively high pitched and a squeaky, rollicking 'orr-uck' is typical with a frequent 'yock-yock-yock'.

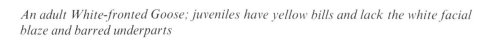

An adult White-fronted Goose; juveniles have yellow bills and lack the white facial blaze and barred underparts

Birds of Estuaries

The introduction (page 7) stresses and explains the great diversity of habitat provided by an estuary and how it is affected by changes in water-cover, water-levels and salinity twice a day and in cyclic changes once a month in the intensity of these changes. A good estuary, and that is one not yet destroyed and polluted by industrial use and abuse, therefore attracts birds of almost every kind at some time or another. The most important special habitats are mud and salting and the most numerous birds, in both species and individuals adapted to either or both, are the waders. This is a very large group of a few related families in which most of the members have slender, more or less long bills for probing in mud and similarly long legs for doing so in the most profitable place — just behind rising or ebbing tides. Length of bill and length of leg correspond quite closely in tidal feeders but not in the Snipe which can almost squat and insert its bill to the hilt in marsh mud without getting its body wet. Tideline feeders lessen competition amongst themselves by being adapted to feeding at different depths, and therefore different distances, from the precise edge of the water. They may often be seen feeding together at the edge of a steep-sided gully or on wet mud but they spread into zones where the crowding is greatest, at mid-tide on gently sloping mud. If it is sandy and Sanderlings happen to be there, these short-legged, short-billed birds bustle about right on the margin. Just in the water the slightly longer billed and longer legged Dunlins crowd, perhaps with some Turnstones. Knot feed in the same zone but pack densely in their own areas. In the next zone, where the water is up to about 10cm deep the Redshanks are active and towards the outer edge, Bar-tailed Godwits. The Black-tailed Godwits have longer legs although there is little difference in the length of bill, and they are in a band beyond the Redshanks, together with Whimbrels and perhaps Greenshanks. The outermost zone is the preserve of the

Curlews. Gulls, of course, paddle or swim at all depths. Avocets may be with the Curlews and Ruff with the Redshanks but neither is commonly a tideline feeder, both preferring pools in saltings and grassland.

Another wading bird, but not a 'wader', is the Heron and this is commonly seen in salting gutters or out on the mud, particularly outside the breeding season. The ditches and fields at the edges of saltings, where bushes and long grass provide low cover, are favourite haunts of the Reed Bunting. The Grey Plover, Ringed Plover, Turnstone and Oystercatcher will follow the tide when not much mud has yet been uncovered but they prefer to pick about on gutter-sides, reefs with bladder-wrack and patches of mud.

Grey Heron

Ardea cinerea

It is remarkable that such a large, slow and vulnerable bird, often persecuted by angling interests, should not only survive but breed in every county and maintain its numbers. Severe winters are the cause of big declines, to half the breeding pairs or less, but despite pollution and disturbance of feeding waters and some felling of woods used for nesting, the numbers return to normal in a few years. In 1963 the Grey Heron was reduced to about 2000 pairs and in 1978 probably over 7000 pairs bred. Where possible the heronries are in mature trees, often oak but there are some in willows and Scots Pine. Where there are no trees the nests are in reed-beds, on cliffs or in low bushes. Herons are particularly fond of eels for food and these give the birds some trouble with the excess of oily mucus. Jelly-like deposits regurgitated by herons can be found on bogs, and to clean mucus from the feathers herons have 'powderdown' areas on their backs, sides and on the lower breast, where down feathers break into a powder; the claw of the middle toe has comb-like projections to remove the powder which has soaked up the oil. To catch its food the Heron has a long neck, strongly muscled, and a big bill. These are heavy and in flight the head has to be drawn back near to the shoulders to preserve the balance. The long legs project well beyond the tail and the hind claw can be seen from quite a distance pointing upwards. The harsh call, 'Fraank' rings across the marshes.

Grey Mullet abound in many estuaries, providing rich feeding for the Heron

Oystercatcher
Haematopus ostralegus

The pursuit of oysters has no part in this bird's life for, in fact, it feeds on mussels, cockles and limpets among shell-fish, and worms, crabs and insect larvae. Although found along any sort of coastline, it is the muddy estuaries which attract Oystercatchers in big flocks. At high tide ten thousand birds may rest together on a reef or islet or pack on a nearby field. As the receding tide uncovers the mud they will return in several large straggling flocks with a great deal of piping, flapping their rather broad wings rapidly but shallowly, giving an easy-looking flight. Every so often a 'piping party' will be held on the mud and the birds run around with their bills forward emitting a rippling chorus of the loud, clear 'kleep-kleep' call running into 'pik-a-pik-a-pik-a . . .'. Oystercatchers breed throughout Scotland and are familiar there on inland pastures and moors in the same way as are Lapwings. This extension from shore-bird to farmland bird is spreading southwards and now reaches to mid-Lancashire and is becoming noticeable in East Anglia. In the rest of England, as in Wales and Ireland, it breeds by the shore in every suitable place, but such places decline in numbers with the spread of holiday-making to hitherto undisturbed parts. In breeding plumage, the white collar disappears and the black extends unbroken from the crown to the breast. Non-breeding birds spend the summer in numbers in areas of saltings and mud. Inland breeding birds move to the coast by the autumn and some Oystercatchers winter in Spain and North Africa.

A resting group of Oystercatchers, or Sea-pies as they are known locally. The white collars indicate winter plumage

Ringed Plover
Charadrius hiaticula

A pleasant 'tew-y' calls attention to two or three very small waders flying fast along the shore, their narrow wings flickering and showing a white bar. The shore can be sandy, rocky or mud and salting but these Ringed Plover will be there. They will often be flying with a few Turnstones or Dunlin but upon settling they will feed solitarily. Estuaries with mud among wrack-covered rocks will hold several hundreds of the birds: at high water they will pack together to rest on a reef or field but feeding they are thinly scattered everywhere. They look compact and round-headed with a short bill and, like other plovers, they make short runs with their bodies level and tilt over when they stop to put their bill in the mud. This bird breeds around the coast in most places, moving into sanctuaries as disturbance spreads along the favoured sandy and pebbly shores. It also breeds inland, particularly in southern Scotland but also in the north, in central Ireland and in East Anglia. Inland nests are on river, reservoir or lakeside shingle in the north and, increasingly in the south, by gravel-pits and the pools near power-stations. At such places and on sandy shores of lakes small numbers of Ringed Plovers will spend a few days on spring or autumn passage. The song is a musical, lilting, skirling sound building up from the call-note to a climax and then fading away, 'tew-y, tew-y, tew-witu-tuwituweeo-tuwituweeo . . .'.

Cockle shells and small stones are often arranged around the perimeter of the Ringed Plover's nest scrape

Kentish Plover
Charadrius alexandrinus

Like the Manx Shearwater, Dartford Warbler and Sandwich Tern, the Kentish Plover no longer breeds in the area from which it was originally named. The Kentish Plover takes it further—it no longer breeds anywhere in Britain and the few nesting in the Channel Islands become fewer every year as bungalows and dog-running invade their territory. Until 1930 a few pairs bred regularly behind the barbed wire of a military enclosure near Dungeness and until 1956 there were occasional nests in Sussex and Suffolk, but since then there have been none. It was a summer visitor, arriving in mid-April and departing in late September and, apart from the handful of birds coming to breed, there were, as now, rare passage migrants in late spring and early autumn. Muddy estuaries and salting-edges are the most likely places in which to see one, in Norfolk or Kent but sometimes north to Yorkshire and west to the Isles of Scilly. Taking the world as a whole, the Kentish Plover is probably the most widespread of all waders, breeding in North and South America, Australia, Tasmania, Ceylon, Japan and across Central Siberia to Europe and Africa.

A pair of Kentish Plovers in breeding plumage, the male in the foreground

Grey Plover
Pluvialis squatarola

Pale brownish from a distance in winter, seen more closely the
Grey Plover is beautifully marked, but in its summer plumage
it is from any viewpoint a dazzlingly handsome bird. Since the
bird breeds only in the high Arctic it is only briefly that we see
it with its face and underside jet black, when some of the birds
wintering here moult early just before leaving in April, and a
few fully moulted birds pass through in May. In winter, a
flying Grey Plover is a round-headed, short-billed and sharp-
winged bird like the Golden Plover although with a rather
faint pale wing-bar, but it is at once distinguished by a large
black oval patch under the root of the wing. The Grey Plover
is found on muddy estuaries, preferably with saltings (deeply
guttered grasslands flooded by the highest tides), well-scattered
when feeding but flying in small parties. In the Chichester
harbour area they can be seen in hundreds but elsewhere
twenty or thirty is a big flock. No bird does the short rapid run
ending in a forward tilt more markedly than the Grey Plover.
They call quite freely when flying and their note seems just
right for a desolate place on a wild day. It has a plaintive and
slightly grating quality hard to capture in letters, but it can be
written as 'scree-oo-ee' or 'sche-wee'.

*Preparing to land, a pair of Grey Plover in winter plumage, showing their
characteristic black axillaries*

Turnstone
Arenaria interpres

This bird does earn its name, and in its careful working over the shore for food it will turn over large pebbles for its favourite diet, sandhoppers. However, it is more usually seen parting or lifting fronds of wrack as it works slowly over reefs, harbour-walls and rocks at the foot of a cliff. It breeds well to the north of the British Isles, all round the north polar regions, but is found on our coasts at all times mainly as a winter visitor and on passage, and many non-breeding birds stay for the summer. Unfortunately these are not in their brilliantly black, white and russet breeding plumage, which is seen only in birds about to depart in May. However, the winter plumage is pleasantly and distinctively particoloured and the small flocks, which rise from the wrack as the tide prevents further feeding, show a well marked black and white pattern. On rising the birds make their hard 'trittrittrit' call and when they settle quite a chorus of chittering arises. But once down they can be quite hard to see on shingle or amongst rocks because of their broken colour pattern. Like other arctic breeders, the Turnstones return from their brief spell in the continuous daylight of the far north after the round-the-clock, mid-July to October duties of family raising are completed, adults mostly coming first.

A Turnstone in winter plumage feeds avidly on sandhoppers (Gammarus), *common amongst tideline debris*

Little Stint

Calidris minuta

The standard 'small wader' is the Dunlin, which is almost always conveniently present for comparisons, and is about the same size as a Skylark. The Little Stint is only the size of a Great Tit so this is a field character which is often of use, usually providing the first indication that the bird is something other than a Dunlin, which it resembles in miniature. It can also be recognised by its bright plumage and pure white breast, and by its short, straight bill. The voice too is distinct as the Little Stint calls 'tit' or 'tit-tit-tit', and this is a sharper, harder note than that of the Sanderling and quite different from that of the Dunlin. The Little Stint is more active and quicker in its movements than the Dunlin. It rarely stops to probe with its bill but picks from the surface, and it is very fast in flight. In the spring Little Stints are decidedly scarce birds of passage but in the autumn, beginning in early August, they are easier to find, although in small numbers with strongly marked annual variations. They are often found with Curlew-Sandpipers which arrive at the same time and frequent the same habitats. These are pools in saltings and mud or in flooded seaside meadows, and, less commonly, inland sewage farms and muddy pools in marshes. A few remain through the winter.

A Little Stint in its first autumn plumage stabs at a Kelp fly. In its second autumn the plumage will be more grey

Dunlin

Calidris alpina

If there are any waders along a stretch of shore some Dunlins
are almost certain to be there although they greatly prefer
plain mud and there will be few of them in rocky areas that
have little wrack or on pure sand or shingle beaches. In
estuaries and harbours with plenty of mud they feed along the
edge of the tide in loose flocks usually about 50 to 500 in each,
with much flying in straggling groups along the water's edge. If
there are reefs of low wrack-covered rock they will be scattered
in ones and twos among the Ringed Plover, feeding mostly on
exposed mud amongst the seaweed. They are restless and
waddle busily about, rather hunched as they probe, always apt
to fly off, calling 'skeep!' which persuades others to rise and
join them. In late spring single notes are sometimes run into
the purring trill which forms their song. Our wintering birds
breed in the Arctic but in April about 5,000 pairs from further
south arrive in Britain to breed, for this is their most southerly
breeding place in the world. The few that now breed on
Dartmoor are at the extreme limit, and there are a few in
Wales and in Ireland, but the bulk of them nest in the Pennines
and the northern Highlands. They are little seen on the moors
since they are few and in the remoter parts, and they all leave
in July before most of the tourists arrive. In April and May the
breeding plumage, with rich browns on the back and black on
the lower breast, is seen on many birds by the coast.

A small group of winter Dunlin preening and 'cat-napping'

Knot

Calidris canutus

Although the call of this bird has the sound of 'knut', there is no need for the 'k' there and the name surely derives, as is implied by the second Latin name, from King Canute or Knut. His legendary demonstration to his court that the tide cannot be defied is commonly grossly distorted and the poor man made to sound a fool, but this bird can be said daily to show Canute's real attitude. It is normally seen massed along the tideline feeding in the shallow water in one large, dense pack or herded immobile, like a grey rug, over bars or reefs just clear of high water. In big bays with muddy rivers weaving across at low tide, like The Wash, the mouth of the Dee and the Lancashire coast, feeding flocks can cover half a mile of water's edge. They rise as a single flock, streaming into the air like rising steam and with a roar of wings audible from afar. They may spend the high water period, when feeding areas are covered, flying to and fro over the water. There are so many accounts of the remarkable instantaneous turns of huge flocks like these that observers think that is what they are seeing, but in fact the feature of Knot flocks at a distance is the way the brownish, smoke-like mass when they are showing their upper sides turns sparkling white, like a wave passing along the flock, as the undersides come into view. Spitsbergen is the closest place to Britain where Knots breed and few are seen here in summer. Single birds or twos and threes are not uncommon by inland reservoirs and lakes.

Knot feeding on a major food item, the bivalve Macoma. Small pellets of pink Macoma shells are cast by the bird

Ruff

Philomachus pugnax

The Ruff, like the Shag, wears the adornment from which it derives its name only very briefly and, since few breed here, it is seen even less often appropriately plumed. The status of the Ruff has changed very much for the better in the last thirty years. It was a fairly rare passage migrant seen only in autumn and spring after about 1870, when regular breeding ceased. Then by 1950 small numbers spent the winter on London Airport and soon more were wintering in south coast estuaries. By 1963 it was breeding again in Norfolk and in the next ten years it bred in four or five other counties. In 1978 one Sussex harbour held a single winter flock of over 400 birds. The female, or Reeve, shown here, is very like the male when he is not in breeding plumage and both are identifiable rather negatively as almost Redshank-sized waders with shortish bills and no conspicuous white or other markings but usually yellow legs. However, in both autumn and spring there are occasional males in partial moult and these are variously but unmistakably particoloured, usually black and white about the head. The males on the breeding grounds have large ruffs and ear-tufts, and these are black, white, dark purple, chestnut or brown, plain, mottled or barred. They gather on display grounds where there are elaborate courtship displays and fights and the Reeves come for mating only, without forming pairs for rearing the young.

A Reeve in winter plumage; the male Ruff is a larger, stockier version of the female

Sanderling
Calidris alba

This Dunlin-sized bird is at all times easily distinguishable from the Dunlin and differs in almost every feature although they are often seen together. Dunlin may join the Sanderlings but seldom the other way round, for the Sanderling stays largely on wide, sweeping beaches and sand-bars and on the seaward side of saltings rather than the muddy creeks preferred by the Dunlin. Flying together in winter in small flocks, they are at once separable as the Sanderling appears almost white all over and has a prominent white, black-edged wing-bar. Its call is very distinct, a sharp 'twik-twik'. Large flocks, seen only by long, open beaches, are all Sanderlings with perhaps a few temporarily connected Oystercatchers. Feeding is mainly at the edge of the tide and is done always at the double, almost in a frenzy, the little black feet a blur as the birds rush into the shallow water and out again between the waves or run along the edge. On small beaches a dozen or so Sanderlings may feed with a few Ringed Plover, Turnstones or Oystercatchers; when someone approaches, the other waders fly off but the Sanderlings may be quite confiding, only taking off to swing out over the water and returning to the beach further along when the disturber is a dozen paces away. Sanderlings breed only in the high arctic, from Spitsbergen across Siberia and Canada to Greenland, but they migrate as far as Chile, South Africa and Australia. Breeding plumage may be seen on birds passing north in May, when inland lakes are visited early in the morning. The head, back and breast are light chestnut, mottled black, and the belly is pure white.

A Sanderling in winter plumage. The summer plumage is a contrast of rust upper parts and white belly

110

Redshank
Tringa totanus

No bird is more the essence of a day on the saltings, summer or winter, in sight and in sound, than the Redshank. Being both restless and noisy as well as numerous, its presence is obvious all day. Single birds rise from hidden pools, small parties from creeks and larger flocks move to and from the shoreline as the tide rises or falls. The old wildfowlers disliked the 'Warden of the Marshes', as they called it, for alerting the other birds to their presence with its ringing 'Tee-o-toe-toe!' as it rose in front of them. When less alarmed it calls a clear but slightly mournful 'tee-uw' or a sharper 'tuke', and more upset than usual it starts off with sharp, clattering double notes before subsiding into the other calls. In the spring it scolds with a long series of 'cheep' or 'tuke' notes and when breeding it sits on posts calling 'clee-o, clee-o . . .' and flies around with a rapid 'tu-tu-tu . . .' as a song. It flies fast with rapid jerks of its angular wings, showing much white but this white disappears when it settles. Although most of the breeding-sites are in the moorlands of Scotland and northern England and by coastal marshes in Eastern England, inland water-meadows from Dorset to Yorkshire are widely used by small numbers until drainage and river-management schemes destroy these once lovely places.

A winter Redshank piping its alarm call from a vantage point over the saltings. In summer, the upper plumage is browner, streaked with black

Greenshank
Tringa nebularia

The elegant Greenshank differs from the Redshank in much more than the colour of its legs. It dispenses with all that bird's fuss and lives relatively calmly. When it needs to sound the alarm it does so with a low-pitched loud clear 'tew, tew' once, occasionally twice, and flies steadily away to settle quietly. In flight it is highly distinctive with uniformly black-brown wings between which is a long clear white oval from the lower back to the root of the tail. In winter the strikingly white face and neck show from a distance when it is settled. Many now winter by muddy shores and estuaries but passage migrants in spring and autumn are as often seen at inland sewage farms, reservoirs and lakes and briefly by small pools and flooded fields. They are usually only single birds or up to three or four and flocks of above ten are rare anywhere. Because of the long bill, feeding birds do not need to stoop noticeably unless probing deeply and they often feed by running through shallow water, swinging the bill from side to side, just the tip under water, when small fry can be seen rippling ahead of them. Somewhere around 500 pairs breed from Perthshire northwards in forest bogs, edges of open woodland and on wet rocky slopes. They arrive in early April and the adults leave by July. Many winter in central Africa and our winter birds probably come from Scandinavia and Russia.

A Greenshank preens its winter plumage

Black-tailed Godwit
Limosa limosa

The history of this elegant bird in Britain closely parallels that of the Ruff. Both declined as breeding birds with the drainage of the fens until they were seen here only as none too plentiful autumn and spring birds of passage. Both began to winter here after 1940 in increasing numbers and then began to breed again and are spreading and increasing. The Black-tailed Godwit winter flocks built up to hundreds first by 1950 along the River Shannon in Ireland and by 1960 in Hampshire. Now about 60 pairs breed, mainly on the Ouse Washes but a few in various parts north to the Solway. With their long legs, these godwits feed a little further out on the tide-covered mud than the Dunlins and Knot, towards or among the Curlews. Standing on the look-out after an alarm from a Redshank, they show their long, slender almost straight bills. When they take to flight the bill projecting ahead is balanced by the legs held close together projecting well beyond the tail. In flight they also immediately show the most distinctive feature, a largely black wing with a long, prominent white bar almost reaching the tip. In summer they have a reddish breast. On the wing they are noisy in a quiet way, babbling softly and some giving the clear 'di-duer-di-di' flight-call. They like flat muddy coasts with saltings and inland, wide rivers and lakes bordered by grassland liable to flooding.

Bar-tailed Godwits (*Limosa lapponica*) are similar to their relatives, but they are birds more of shore than of estuary, of mud than of grassland, and breed in the high Arctic. They have an upturned bill longer than the Black-tailed's, and no white bar on the wings.

Black-tailed Godwits, showing the rust-coloured summer plumage which is beginning to appear as individual feathers on neck and breast. Above; a pair of Bar-tailed Godwits

Curlew
Numenius arquata

This fine big bird with the haunting voice is surprisingly widespread in its breeding. Around 50,000 pairs breed in every county west of a line from the Isle of Wight to Hull and in several more east of that line. Most of the nests are on hill-grazing, moors and bogs but in the southeast a few breed on the less frequented commons with boggy areas. These inland areas are used by the Curlew between February and July and during the remainder of the year the birds are to be found on saltings and mudflats. The song ranks as one of the most thrilling of all bird sounds, building up through a long series of 'coor, coor . . .' notes, low and slow at first, rising and accelerating to a climax when it breaks into cascades of bubbling trills, sinking gradually back to the low note. Although song is most intense on the breeding ground it is, fortunately, also heard frequently along the shore and sometimes in every month. On rising, Curlews call a loud 'quoi-quoi' but once on the wing the usual call is that best rendered by the French name for the bird, 'courlis'. When the movements from coast to breeding sites occur, in spring and midsummer, this call can be heard from the night sky even in large cities. Flocks along flat coasts can hold two thousand birds but they straggle and break up frequently. During extra high tides standing Curlews often spend the time in packs on grazing land some distance from the shore.

Shore crabs occasionally form part of a Curlew's diet but the long, curved bill is better suited to probing for worms

Whimbrel

Numenius phaeopus

This smaller, northern edition of the Curlew is also known as the Titterel and the May Whistler from its call and from the time when it is heard most widely. The name 'whimbrel' is probably not directly derived from the 'titterel' call but from 'whimmerel' the whimpering bird. The call, often first heard in the night sky inland, is a clear, loud, evenly emphasised, rippling, 'tee-tee-tee-tee-tee'. There are usually five or six notes, but seven is a mystic number so another name for the bird was 'Seven Whistler'. A few Whimbrel breed on the Scottish mainland and a few more on the Outer Hebrides but the majority of the small population breeds in the Shetland Islands. Very much larger numbers arrive on the south coast in mid-April and pass gradually northwards to their breeding grounds which extend all round the Arctic. Some non-breeders stay with us all the summer and there is an increasing tendency for a few to winter here. They are most numerous in September in flocks of four or five or as single birds, sometimes amongst Curlews but usually on their own. They tend to separate from Curlews as they are much more confiding than that very wary bird. The two birds frequent the same saltings, mud and fields but Whimbrel are found relatively more often than Curlews, and with Oystercatchers on rocky shores. The striped head and shorter, less strongly curved bill distinguish them from Curlews as also does their more rapid wing-action.

A late migrant, the Whimbrel, arrives in Britain well into May and can often be seen flying overhead on its way to the breeding grounds in the north

120

Avocet

Recurvirostra avosetta

The name Avocet which seems to promise an interesting origin is in fact nothing more than 'elegant bird' from the Italian 'avosetta' a diminutive of 'avis' a bird where 'elegant' rather than 'small' is implied. It is, however a highly appropriate name as far as it goes and this dazzlingly black and white, blue-legged bird is always a rewarding sight. Its history in Britain is very like that of the Ruff and Black-tailed Godwit and its re-colonisation of Suffolk coastal marshes was similarly dependent upon huge increases in numbers in Holland and Denmark together with sanctuaries suitable for breeding. These must be coastal marshes with mud islands in brackish water and usually need to be managed by sluices, so Avocet colonies cannot be very numerous or large, and are vulnerable to poor years or disasters from freak tides, storms and floods. By 1840, regular breeding had ceased in former colonies from Romney Marsh to the River Trent. There were isolated nestings in County Wexford, Norfolk and Essex after 1937 and in 1947 four pairs nested at Havergate Island, Suffolk. A managed sanctuary was created and by 1957 there were 97 pairs there, which seems to be about the maximum number for the site as it has not, so far, been exceeded. Overflow is taken by Minsmere where there were 53 pairs in 1977. The call is a clear rather high-pitched 'klooit', often made when birds are flying away, and turning into the more rapid note of alarm, 'klit-klit-klit'. In recent years small parties have been spending the winters in some estuaries along the south coast. Resting birds may sit down or stand with their heads under their wings. Avocets feed by wading in shallow water and swinging the bill from side to side just under or on the surface.

Avocet chicks have straight bills at first and feed themselves soon after hatching, but the curved bill becomes apparent after a few days

Common Snipe

Capella gallinago

The first sight of a Common Snipe is often when it rises
suddenly almost from underfoot by a little pool or a ditch.
With a cry of 'scape!' it zigzags away, rapidly gaining height
on flickering angular wings. It will often then be seen circling
at a fair height, short-bodied with a disproportionately long
bill held pointing well downwards. In flooded fields and at a
few favourable open marshes or muddy pools several hundred
may be watched feeding, probing with the full length of the
bill. On the ground, the bill seems over-long for such a small
bird and is slanted down from its hunched body. The broad,
pale, yellow-brown stripes along each side of the body show up
amongst the grass and they can often be seen on a bird in flight
when the pale hind edge of the wing also shows well. The
Common Snipe has one vocal song and one mechanical song.
In spring it will 'chip-chop' endlessly from the ground or a
perch, especially after dark, the rhythmic notes coming and
going in strength. The mechanical song is part of the display
and can only be made in flight. The bird circles several
hundred feet from the ground, mainly in fine, still weather
soon after dawn and before and during dusk, and suddenly
descends at a steep angle but with the body level for two or
three seconds before regaining height. During the descent a
remarkable trembling, resonant bleating 'wahwahwah-
wahwah' is heard. The outer tail feathers can be seen standing
clear of the others and it is the buzzing of these feathers in
the turbulent air from the winnowed wings that makes this
sound. It resembles somewhat the bleat of a goat, from which
circumstance the bird is called 'Capella', the little goat.

*Remaining motionless, relying on its cryptic colouring, a Common Snipe merges
with the background*

Reed Bunting
Emberiza schoeniclus

This is the only common bunting frequenting reeds, but its name was never very apt, for there are always more birds around the margins than actually in the reed-beds and far more in wet bushy places with long grass and along ditches. When many fields in dry farmland still had their marl-pits, each tiny pool with its hawthorn bush held a pair of Moorhens and a pair of Reed Buntings. Since then, despite most of these pits being filled in, this bird has spread widely on to farm fields and heaths and commons, and even to downland scrub and young conifer plantations, as numbers have increased. The cock starts to sing in mid-February from near the top of a bush and with such a short, feeble song can make his presence felt only by repeating it at very frequent intervals. It starts in a halting manner and ends just when it sounds as though it is getting under way. It can be represented by 'zink, zink, zink-tweedledidee'. The call note, usually given freely in flight, is a sharp 'tseep'. The dark, brown-streaked female is sparrow-like, but as she flies away the black tail with white outer feathers shows her to be a bunting. Breeding is remarkably widespread for a bird associated until recently with wet-lands and the only gaps of any significance are the Cotswold and Wiltshire beechwoods and small areas of the highest Pennines and Grampians. Gravel-pits and canal-banks are favourite haunts of this bird.

A boldly marked male Reed Bunting in summer plumage proclaims ownership of his territory

Index

Avocet 123
Bunting, Reed 126
Chough 69
Cormorant 50
Curlew 119
Dove, Rock 65
Dunlin 105
Eider 75
Fulmar 42
Gannet 49
Godwit, Bar-tailed 117
  Black-tailed 117
Goose, Barnacle 84
  Brent 82
  White-fronted 86
Greenshank 115
Guillemot 56
  Black 58
Gull, Blackheaded 21
  Common 26
  Great Black-backed 22
  Herring 18
  Lesser Black-backed 25
Heron, Grey 91
Kittiwake 28
Knot 106
Mallard 79
Oystercatcher 92
Peregrine 62
Petrel, Storm 47
Pintail 76
Pipit, Rock 67

Plover, Grey 98
  Kentish 97
  Ringed 94
Puffin 60
Razorbill 55
Redshank 112
Reeve 109
Ruff 109
Sanderling 110
Scoter, Common 73
Shag 53
Shearwater, Manx 44
Shelduck 80
Skua, Arctic 38
  Great 37
Snipe, Common 124
Stint, Little 103
Tern, Common 32
  Little 31
  Sandwich 34
Turnstone 100
Whimbrel 120